Pastor Nanthan Dauda Madaki

Leading Unbelievers to Christ

A Guide for Every Christian's Involvement

Blessed Hope Publishing

Imprint

Any brand names and product names mentioned in this book are subject to trademark, brand or patent protection and are trademarks or registered trademarks of their respective holders. The use of brand names, product names, common names, trade names, product descriptions etc. even without a particular marking in this work is in no way to be construed to mean that such names may be regarded as unrestricted in respect of trademark and brand protection legislation and could thus be used by anyone.

Cover image: www.ingimage.com

Publisher:
Blessed Hope Publishing
is a trademark of
International Book Market Service Ltd., member of OmniScriptum Publishing Group
17 Meldrum Street, Beau Bassin 71504, Mauritius

Printed at: see last page
ISBN: 978-613-7-82026-1

LEADING UNBELIEVERS TO CHRIST:
A Guide for Every Christian's Involvement

By

PASTOR NATHAN DAUDA MADAKI

EDITOR
Rev. Manasseh H. Panpe PhD.

LEADING UNBELIEVERS TO CHRIST:
A Guide for Every Christian's Involvement

By
PASTOR NATHAN DAUDA MADAKI

EDITOR
Rev. Manasseh H. Panpe PhD.

BLESSED
HOPE
PUBLISHING
is an imprint of
OmniScriptum GmbH & Co. KG
Bahnhofstr. 28
66111 Saarbrücken
Germany

TABLE OF CONTENTS

Table of Contents	-	-	-	-	-	i
Foreword -	-	-	-	-	-	iv
Dedication	-	-	-	-	-	v
Preface	-	-	-	-	-	vi
Acknowledgment	-	-	-	-	-	vii
Introduction -	-	-	-	-	-	1

One
MAKING THE RIGHT DECISION

Make A Genuine Repentance -	-	-	-	4

Two
BELIEVING THE WORD

Know what you believe	-	-	-	-	9
Know what they believe	-	-	-	-	12

Three
MISSION IN CHRIST'S WAY

Incarnational mission/ministry -	-	-	-	14
Inculturation -	-	-	-	-	19
Identification with the Poor -	-	-	-	21

Mission in the Way of Christ   -   -   -   -   23

Four
EVANGELISM IN DIFFICULT SITUATION

Crisis Evangelism   -   -   -   -   -   25
Types of crisis   -   -   -   -   -   -   26
    Death of a loved one
    Bankruptcy
    Unexpected Failure
    Breakup of a relationship
    Loss of good health

Five
NON-VERBAL APPROACHES TO MISSION

Living an exemplary life   -   -   -   -   30
Dressing   -   -   -   -   -   -   31
    Men Dressing
    Women Dressing
Clothing from an Islamic Perspective   -   -   -   33
Interact with people   -   -   -   -   39
    Family
    Office
    Market
    Generosity

Six
ELEMENTS OF STRAIGHTENING MISSION WORK

Be Prayerful   -   -   -   -   -   50
What is Prayer?-   -   -   -   -   -   50
    Faith
    Worship
    Confession
    Adoration
    Praise

Thanksgiving
Dedicated Action
Request

Seven

RECOGNIZING THE PLAN OF GOD

See them the way God sees them - - - 59

Compassion - - - - - - 61

Eight

UNVEILING THE WORD

Tell them about the good news - - - 64

All have Sinned

The wages of sin is Death

Christ Died for You

You Can Be Saved

Lead them to Christ

Nine

THE CHURCH OBLIGATION

The church and her responsibilities - - - 72

The church should be incarnational

The church should be culturally relevant

The Church should reach the un-reach

The church should preach the sound word

CONCLUSION

Bibliography

FORWARD

n this book, Pastor Nathan Dauda Madaki give attention to one of the essential aspects of Christian responsibility often neglected – the art of sharing the gospel of Jesus Christ for the salvation of unbelievers. While some pastors may teach these to their congregants, nothing much is written for the benefit of the generality.

Madaki provides helpful information especially about Muslims in presenting the gospel to them. He also gave attention to non-verbal approaches like living transformed lives, proper dressing and attitudes that could hinder or aide evangelization. One of the challenges in evangelization is initiation of conversation, in this book Madaki provides some insight to this and also some significant information in sharing Christ cross-culturally and with people affected by various crisis of life.

This book is a good beginning in encouraging every Christian to get involved in evangelization. Anyone having challenges in sharing the good news will be guided by the insight shared in this book.

Rev. Moses Audi, PhD
Baptist Theological Seminary,
Kaduna, NIGERIA

DEDICATION

This book is dedicated to God Almighty for the strength and inspiration He has given me to be part of mission contributors.

PREFACE

People who God had called for mission find it difficult on how and where to start. ***Leading unbelievers to Christ*** is a comprehensive guide to every Christian who does not have the theological or mission and Evangelism training, but wants to lead unbelievers to Christ. This book filled with ideas and experience of mission and missionary work.

Brethren it's a privilege that God has granted you the opportunity to lay your hands on this book material.

ACKNOWLEDGEMENT

I express my profound gratitude to God Almighty for His guidance, provision and protections throughout the period of writing this book. My appreciation goes to my editor President, Rev. Manasseh H. Panpe Phd. for his tireless and sacrificial effort to make this book a success. I also want to specially appreciate Rev. Moses Audi, PhD for writing forward to this book.

My thanks also go to Mrs. Esther L. Solomon and Miss. Linda Dafes for their endurance during the grammar corrections. My appreciation goes to my brothers and sisters Aaron D. Madaki, Pastor Elimelech D. Madaki, Eliezer D. Madaki, and Mrs. Rose Bulus for their love and encouragement.

My appreciation also goes to my parent(s) who train me in the way of the Lord Mrs. Mary Dauda Madaki and Late. Rev. Dauda Madaki Bassahua. To my children, Evelyne Nyambura Madaki, Neariah Nathan Dauda, Micaiah Nathan Dauda, and Adriel Nathan Dauda word can't express my sincere appreciation for your love and prayer may the Almighty God blesses you.

This acknowledgment is null if I didn't express my sincere and profound appreciation to my benevolent, admirable, charming and beautiful wife, Mrs. Gloria N. Madaki, for your love, patience, endurance, payers, encouragement, and support throughout the period of writing this book, I Love you.

Pastor N.D Madaki

INTRODUCTION

Many people find it difficult to win unbelievers to Christ with an excuse, of pushing the job to Pastors, evangelists and missionaries. I will like to draw your attention closer to know that it is every person's (Christian) business to undergo Kingdom investment by investing time, money and properties in other to bring the lost one to the throne of grace. That's why Jesus says:

> *"…'All authority in heaven and on earth has been given to me. Go therefore make disciples of all nations baptizing them in the name of the Father and of the Son and of the Holy Spirit, teaching them to observe all I have commanded you. And behold I am with you always to end of the age"* (Matthew 28:18-20 ESV).

The duty of every Christian is to go and preach the Gospel to unbelievers. The plurality of the word "Disciples" shows that Jesus is expecting more than one disciple from every Christian.

If that is the case, it means you and I have a great task to accomplish whether you are a pastor or not. The work do not have a specific venue or area, wherever you find yourself either by the road side, school, market, office, filling station, football field/club, farm, restaurant etc. You can use that opportunity you have to lead the unbeliever to Christ. I know many people who say: I am not a pastor I don't know how to start talking to unbelievers about Christ, to some they say, they don't have the knowledge or time to go for the training.

Thank God Almighty who use and help me to convert this Inspiration into a book that will serve as a guideline to every mission minded Christian who does not have the basic training on pastoral and mission/evangelism to win unbelievers to Christ. No matter your field, position, occupation you find yourself. This book is an opportunity to the present-day Christian's communities who are willing to work for God and are willing to lead unbelievers to Christ.

This book comes at the right time and situation where the Church is facing hardship in the hands of unbelievers. If as Christians you cannot preach, teach and mentor unbelievers; then it means you are going back to your creator empty handed. These unbelievers are very ignorance of their behavior and actions, because they did not have the knowledge of God in them. They will use their ignorance to punish or kill believers. The most unfortunate of thing is that church has forgotten Christ's mission on earth which is (The Great Commission (Matthew 28:19-20). We always embark on building mansions instead of mission, and this mansions has become the major priority of today's church; thank God for giving you the work of reconciling others to Christ. Do you remember the story of Jonah whom God sent to Nineveh? God said;

> **"Go to the great city of Nineveh and preach against it, because its wickedness has come up before me"** *Jonah 1:2 NIV.*

Jonah did not want to do the work God assigned him and God remind him of his assignment and he do God's assignment successfully. Don't forget that the primary purpose of the church on earth is to carry out the gospel to the whole nations; if the church forgets the mission of Christ on earth, who then will do the work? The work of terrorist groups who are persecuting the church today, reminds the church to be up to her feet and do her responsibilities as a church.

This book is a wakeup call to you to recommit yourself; churches and organizations to fully engage yourself into God's project properly. The church is suffering; the remedy to all terrorist sects is the Word of God.

As you read this book I encourage you to use every opportunity you have with an unbeliever to tell him or her about Jesus Christ.

CHAPTER **1** MAKING THE RIGHT DECISION

Genuine Repentance

A sinner cannot save a sinner, as it is said; a blind man cannot lead a blind man; they will all fall into a pit (Matthew 15:14). But if you are not a genuine Christian, then you are an unbeliever; many people find themselves into Christianity by luck (because their parents are Christians). This will not qualified you to become a Christian; the Bible says:

> "But to all who received him, who believed in his name, he gave power to become children of God" (John 1:12 RSV).

You can't be a Christian without accepting and believing Christ as your personal Lord and Saviour. If you didn't accept and believe in Christ, going to church has no impact to your future life. Stop deceiving yourself that your parents are Christians or your father is a clergy. I want you to know that Christianity is not a heritable rite or religion; it is a religion that you have to work for your salvation with fear and trembling. Jesus knew it that is why He said, there would be people who will claim that they are His, but they have not invited or accepted Christ as their personal Lord and Saviour in their lives:

"Not everyone who says to me, 'Lord, Lord,' will enter the kingdom of heaven, but only he who does the will of my Father who is in heaven" (Matt. 7:21 NIV)

The outward profession of religion will not take one to heaven; many church gowers, think that since they have engaged themselves in church activities, they claim to be genuine Christians; NO, it does not happen like that. Jesus said you must first accept Him as your personal Lord and Savior. This means you must be a born again Christian Jesus said to Nicodemus "I tell you the truth, no one can see the kingdom of God unless he is born again." (John 3:3 NIV) How can one be born again? Nicodemus ask:

Surely he cannot enter a second time into his mother's womb to be born! Jesus answered, "I tell you the truth, no one can enter the kingdom of God unless he is born of water and the Spirit. Flesh gives birth to flesh, but the Spirit gives birth to spirit. You should not be surprised at my saying, 'You must be born again.' (John 3:4-8 NIV)

Jesus emphasized about being born again; you will never get access to heaven unless you are a genuine Christian (born again). Confess your sin and accept Christ as your personal Lord and Saviour. Though your face would not change but your life will change spiritually.

That's why Apostle Paul says:

> This means that anyone who belongs to Christ has become a new person. The old life is gone; a new life has begun! (2Co 5:17 NLT)

You cannot become a new person unless you put your sinful nature to death; putting it to death means you now belong to Christ.

Believe in Him:

Jesus says John 3:16 NIV: "For God so loved the world that he gave his one and only Son, that whoever believes in him shall not perish but have eternal life".

Many so called Christians (church gowers) confess Christ with their mouth but in their heart they have another thought. This will be referred to later.

Jesus is the only way to Heaven, forget about the express way that someone have ever told you, forget about the new churches that deceive you to change your church in other to make your life better, God is not in a church but rather in you. Paul said to the Corinthians:

> "And what union can there be between God's temple and idols? For we are the temple of the living God. As God said: "I will live in them and walk among them. I will be their God, and they will be my people" (2 Cor 6:16) NLT.

❀

6

Invite Jesus today to be the master of your life, and your life will never remain the same. Stick to the church you find yourself before; that's why Paul reminds Timothy:

> "They will betray their friends, be reckless, be puffed up with pride, and love pleasure rather than God. They will act religious, but they will reject the power that could make them godly. Stay away from people like that! They are the kind who work their way into people's homes and win the confidence of vulnerable women who are burdened with the guilt of sin and controlled by various desires. (Such women are forever following new teachings, but they are never able to understand the truth.) These teachers oppose the truth just as Jannes and Jambres opposed Moses. They have depraved minds and a counterfeit faith". (2Tim. 3:4-8 NLT)

The questions are, where are these churches right from inception? Where are these teachings coming from? Are their teachings Biblical and doctrinally sound? Why can't they go to the villages to win the missing souls to Christ and add members to their church? I believe if the Spirit of the Lord is with you, God will reveal to you who they are; and how to interact with them.

7

God loves you that's why He sent His son to save you from the bondage of sin. If you are able to go and share the Gospel of Christ salvation free of charge, then why can't you go and aid those who are willing to go and preach the gospel to those who are still living in darkness? Whoever you maybe, whatever is your position in life, search yourself whether you are a genuine Christian or not; if you are not then invite Jesus into your live today and He will help you. Believe me you will go beyond expectation here on earth and you'll live in abundant blessing and your life will never remain the same.

CHAPTER **2** BELIEVING THE WORD

Know what you believe

"For God so loved the world, that he gave his only begotten Son, that whosoever <u>believeth</u> in him should not perish, but have everlasting life" (John 3:16 KJV)

The above scripture gives us choice to have everlasting life or permanent condemnation. Many people who claim to be Christians don't know the commitment and the promise behind this verse. Today, most unbelievers watch the life of other believers to see whether what Christians believe on, will lead them to eternity or not. This remains me of one of our mission outreach where an unbeliever was asking about the Trinity; the young man ask one of the team members, "is this trinity means you are worshiping three gods?" The team members answered N O, are you saying that Jesus is God?" A team member said, yes another team member said no. An argument arose between the team members; and they departed without giving the unbeliever a genuine answer. When we met in the evening to pray and evaluate performances, a group team secretary reported what happened during evangelism and mission and it was discovered that, she did not know what she believed in; and made us started another training again in the mission field. It is important to note that every member of Christ's body who is going to the mission field, evangelism or outreach should undergo thorough training and test to enable that person meet up with the task ahead. Before Jesus handed over the mantle of wining souls to his disciples, he trained them for three years, tested them to see if they were fit for the task ahead (Mtt. 10:1),

> When Jesus had called the Twelve together, he gave them power and authority to drive out all demons and to cure diseases, and he sent them out to proclaim the kingdom of God and to heal the sick. He told them: "Take nothing for the journey—no staff, no bag, no bread, no money, no extra shirt. Whatever house you enter, stay there until you leave that town. If people do not welcome you, leave their town and shake the dust off your feet as a testimony against them." So they set out and went from village to village, proclaiming the good news and healing people everywhere. (Lk. 9:1-6).

The Bible did not give us the reports of the twelve disciples sent out (Lk.9:1-6). But Jesus in later chapter Luke 10:1-7 sent out seventy-two set of believers to the town and villages two by two. The second outreach yielded a great result and they came back happy "The seventy-two returned with joy and said, "Lord, even the demons submit to us in your name." (Lk. 10:17). This denotes that the disciples were well equipped and were ready for the task ahead. An experience such this case on that study has helped to seriously plan very well before engaging members into any outreach/evangelism. As the Bible rightly explains that Jesus continues to mentor them until He discovered that they were ready to reach out to the whole nations. The disciples too when they came together they ask him, "Lord, are you at this time going to restore the kingdom to Israel? (Acts 1:8). Don't forget Jesus' disciples were thinking about the worldly kingship, because for long the Israelites were under the Rule of the Romans, therefore they thought that Jesus is going to deliver Israel from the kingdom. But Jesus in his divine wisdom said to his disciples,

> "It is not for you to know the times or dates the Father has set by his own authority. But you will receive power when the Holy Spirit comes on you; and you will be my witnesses in Jerusalem, and in all Judea and Samaria, and to the ends of the earth." (Acts 1:7-9).

If you do not know what you believe, instead of leading people to Christ, they will pull you or confuse the message of the gospel. It is better to know the Bible and the God you are serving or worshiping and become acquitted with it. Many Christians have big study Bibles, and Bible commentaries but they do not study them, they are like pictures in their homes; that is why Paul says:

> "Study to show thyself approved unto God, a workman that needeth not to be ashamed, rightly dividing the word of truth. (2Tim. 2:15 KJV)

Bibles and Bible commentaries are purposefully made for reading and studying to enlighten the reader to know what is expected of him/her. On the other way, some Christians don't have the Bible; if you don't have a Bible, how can you show yourself approved man of God to unbelievers? If you don't study how and where can you get the message for them?

According to (John 3:16), the word believeth. What does it mean by the word believe? According to Oxford Advance Learner's Dictionary, believe is "feeling that something is true or that somebody is telling the truth". Jesus says "...whosoever believes in me shall not perish..." looking at the above definition, if you do not believe and fully feel that what Jesus said and what is written in the Bible is true, you will never win unbelievers.

Know what they believe

Historical Principle is one of the methods used to interpret the New Testament or the Bible. In other to lead unbelievers to Christ, you are required to know their historical life, culture and religion. Knowing their dos and dons of the people is very important in leading unbelievers to Christ. The Bible says:

Then Joshua son of Nun secretly sent two spies from Shittim. "Go, look over the land," he said, "especially Jericho."... (Joshua 2:1 NIV)

Joshua the Chief Commander sent spies to spy Jericho.

Using Joshua's methodology, it's important to know their culture, know what they believe, and know where the Bible is talking on what they believed on.

Before you finish asking an unbeliever these questions as you're praying for God's intervention, God will give you the grace and opportunity to start talking to him or her about Christ. Don't forget that there are different types of religions and cultures; you can apply these questions in difference ways, it depends on the area, culture and environment you may find yourself.

CHAPTER 3 MISSION IN CHRIST'S WAY

1. Incarnational Mission/Ministry

Glann Rogers: define incarnational mission and ministry as, *"being involve or becoming, as fully as possible, one of the people to whom you go to preach the gospel"*. It involves learning the culture and language of the local people so you can see the world through their eyes, seeing what they see from their point of view, so you can address their needs in a way that is relevant to them. It is not good for someone who is leading unbelievers to Christ to start by condemning their culture, food, dressing and their lives; it will be even good to eat the food they eat if it is not against the Christian doctrine. This will encourage them to listen to you the more and they will also feel that you are one of them.

This is my experience some years ago as a young Pastor which may be useful to people. I was once in mission-field trip to a village of about 80 to 90 kilometers away from main road; the people have their cultural food they eat. One day I asked a woman to give me some of their food to eat. Another woman with her spoke in their dialect "do you think that pastor will enjoy this food? Please don't put much for him". When they brought the food, I ate all. As I finished eating, one of the people spoke in the language I understand (Hausa) and said: "pastor when you asked of our cultural food, we thought that you may not eat it, but we are amazed when we discovered that you ate our local food". Again he said "but pastor, you are not like other pastors who normally come to our place". To be frank, I involve myself in eating their cultural food and begin to learn their language, their work and other things they do. At the end of my mission work in the village, the people enjoyed my bible teachings and other church programme and when I was to leave the village, the people were crying for my leaving and promise to do what God is expecting from them.

The method I used in this village may not be the same method you ought to use, but you should study the lifestyle of the people and allow God to tell you the method that will work for you in the environment that you may find yourself.

The concept of incarnational mission or ministry is crucial to success in proclaiming the gospel and ministering effectively to God's people in their unique sociocultural context. The idea of incarnational mission and ministry grows out of God's willingness to become human (the incarnation) in order to identify with us, communicate effectively with us, and serve us.

Jesus participated fully in all that it means to live as human life. The marvelous thing is that in Jesus, God Himself began to live a fully human life.

"And the Word became flesh and dwelled among us, and we beheld His glory, glory as of the only Son of the Father, full of grace and truth." (John 1:14)

John 1:14 describes the Incarnation of the Son of God. The Incarnation tells us of Jesus Christ, whom is Devine and human. Word Made Flesh's philosophy of ministry commits us to an "incarnational methodology." But in what sense can we speak of the Incarnation as a methodology for ministry? How are we to imitate God becoming human? It would be wrong to think of a Christian worker as the equivalent of the divine Word coming from the Father to dwell among humans. We are not God; we are not the Word; we are not Christ. Yes, Christ is with us; the Spirit of God dwells among us; but does that say anything "incarnational" about our mission?

The Incarnation demonstrates God's great commitment to all humanity, to live among us and to die on our behalf. But Jesus' very humanity means that God, ironically, has shown us by His own example how to be human. Our faith in Jesus includes a calling to be Christ-like, "to walk just as He walked" (1 John 2:6). This implies, among other things, a similar commitment to be with people, to be present, available to be used by God. This incarnational methodology takes on different aspects.

Starting from the confession that Jesus is the only Son, the divine Word, we will consider the implications of the Incarnation for the mission of the church. Most broadly, this means we will look at Jesus Christ as our role model of ministry and mission, bearing in mind the divine-human dynamic of Christ's two natures. What we mean by "incarnational mission," then, is a commitment to be with people, to embody the good news we preach, and through the Spirit to mediate the presence of Christ wherever He is needed. As the body of Christ, we are the continuation of His ministry; we are His representatives on earth 2Cor. 5:20. We are the salt of the earth Mtt. 5:13, the light of the world Mtt. 5:14. If we are to be faithful to this calling, we don't run away from the world's great need, rather we run to it. We must be willing to lay down our lives and take up the life of God in Christ. Not only has God touched humanity; in Jesus, God was touched by humanity, and by us He was condemned to death. Yet in the Resurrection He triumphed over our judgment on Him and offered in return His forgiveness and grace. We have wounded God, but His love endures. Because of this, Christianity has in various times and places celebrated suffering and persecution; for in losing like this, is being condemned, the saints of past and present have found true life. Their testimony has been, not resentment, but hope and peace. To be incarnational, then, is not just a strategic choice we make simply because we see it as an effective option. It is a calling to follow Jesus with crosses in our hands (Matt. 16:24; 1 Pet. 2:21).

The Incarnation demonstrates God's commitment to humanity. He has not abandoned us to destruction but reaches out in compassion to find a way to save us. As Jesus' disciples, we should take up the same commitment to the salvation and welfare of the people of the world. Ashley Barker and John Hayes, current mission leaders among the poor, reflect:

"Today, perhaps, more than ever, the world needs Christians who allow themselves to not just be seen and heard, but touched and handled. We live in an age of information, of mass messages, and an era with an mysterious ability to multiply words. Yet an increasing number of the world's people live lives without real change and without Christ. The world doesn't need more words, not even more of the 'right' words; the world needs more words made flesh. It is a simple truth, yet in the end it is people who change people. The world needs more people living good news incarnationally in a way they can be seen, heard and handled by the most demanding and doubting Thomas's" (Sub-Merge: Living Deep in a Shallow World).

Jesus show us who the Father is, what God is like. Our lives witness shows what Jesus is like. "As the Father has sent me, so I send you," He told His disciples (John 20:21). Jesus sends us forth, and as we go, we draw on His life, the life of the Incarnation. We don't claim to have arrived, but we press on to become conformed to Christ and thus to be "imitators of God" (Eph. 5:1).

Incarnational mission or ministry involves becoming, as fully as possible, one of the people to whom you go to preach the gospel. It involves learning the culture and language of the local people so you can see the world through their eyes, seeing what they see from their own point of view, so you can address their needs in a way that is relevant to them.

2.   Inculturation

In Christianity, inculturation is the adaptation of the way Church teachings are presented to non-Christian cultures and, in turn, the influence of those cultures on the evolution of these teachings. Many missiologists have taken the Incarnation as a model of "inculturation" of the good news, in which the church is born anew within each culture in a way that fits that culture.

It is easy to pick on missionaries of the past, but do not ignore their real accomplishments and their heroism in leaving their homes in order to bring Christ to the great masses of those who had never heard the Gospel. They built schools and clinics, elevated the status of women, translated the Bible, preserved local languages by developing writing systems and developed leaders without regard to social standing.

The starting point for this approach comes from Jesus' Incarnation into a specific culture. This approach placed Jesus in a specific cultural setting and reflects on Jesus' ability to pursue His mission as a participating member of that culture, teaching and acting in ways that addressed the hopes and dreams of a specific people, even though there are limits to this strategic approach. After all, Jesus was not primarily a matter of strategy, but derived from God's covenant with Abraham and Israel. The emphasis of the Incarnation is not on Jesus' specific culture, but on His humanity.

That is, Jesus did not just appear to be human, and He was human.

Anyone working cross-culturally is always an outsider to some extent. We can approximate the cultural ways of a new culture, but we can never completely shed who we are culturally, with the values, attitudes and ways of seeing the world that have shaped us since infancy.

Jesus and the Samaritan woman is one of the greatest Biblical examples of incarnational mission which is found in the book of John 4:4-41. During the ministry of Christ on earth, it is well known that Jews do not associate with Samaritans. Then, why did Jesus ask the Samaritan woman to give him water? But the woman's answer reminded Jesus of the disunity between the Jews and Samaritans. Jesus' respond to this matter was very interested and captivated. "If you knew the gift of God and who is it that ask you for a drink, you would have asked him and he would have given you living water" (John 4:10 NLT).

The woman mistakenly believed that if she received the water Jesus offered, she would not have to return to the well each day. She was interested in Jesus message because she thought it could make her life easier. But if that were always the case, people would accept Christ's message for the wrong reasons. Christ did not come to take away life challenges, but to change us on the inside and to empower us to deal with problems from God's perspective.

When this woman discovered that Jesus knew all about her private life, she quickly changed the subject. Often, people become uncomfortable when the conversation is too close to home, and they try to talk about something else. As we witness, we should gently guide the conversation back to Christ.

Incanational mission/ministry is one of the best way to witness to people, but it is important to be very careful on how to present the message because at any point you may create problem instead of leading the unbeliever to Christ.

Jesus' Incarnation, then, reminds us that we cannot divorce our witness from the specific cultural context within which it takes place. As humans, we can never be culturally neutral or outside of any culture. Especially in cross-cultural contexts, this can never be forgotten without painful consequences.

3.   Identification with the Poor

A commitment to be with the people takes on special significance when it comes to ministry among the poor. Whether or not our simplicity of lifestyle can be called "poor," we do not share the condition of the truly destitute. We are not forced to draw upon the same resources for bare survival that they are. We need to be humble in this area no matter how great we are. Most of us lead very privileged lives, and as such we have only a limited capacity for trusting God in truly desperate conditions.

For us who are not-poor, to genuinely embrace the poor and embody good news to the poor is always a challenge. We realize our limits and realize what an act of grace it is that God uses us at all. The poor of the world known are often more generous, more hospitable and more community-centered than have ever been. How are we supposed to serve them? It often seems like we are the ones being served.

To serve the poor in the way of the Incarnation means being willing to embrace poverty. It might mean eating things that we would normally throw out as unfit. It might mean coming into contact with filth. It might mean jeopardizing our social standard. The reward is to be with the poor, to enjoy blessed fellowship with the poor, which cannot happen if our fears keep us away. This reminds me of one of our Mission survey in a very remote village. The people offered us food and some of our people rejected the food. The villagers were not happy.

It requires faith to believe that the rewards are worth the sacrifice. Consider the rich young man whom Jesus asked to sell his possessions, give it to the poor and follow Him.

> Someone came to Jesus with this question: "Teacher, what good things must I do to have eternal life?" "Why ask me about what is good?" Jesus replied. "Only God is good. But to answer your question, you can receive eternal life if you keep the commandments." "Which ones?" the man asked. And Jesus replied: " 'Do not murder. Do not commit adultery. Do not steal. Do not testify falsely. Honor your father and mother. Love your neighbor as yourself.'" "I've

obeyed all these commandments," the young man replied. "What else must I do?" Jesus told him, "If you want to be perfect, go and sell all you have and give the money to the poor, and you will have treasure in heaven. Then come, follow me." But when the young man heard this, he went sadly away because he had many possessions". (Matt. 19:16-22 NLT).

If the young man had obeyed, it would be easy to accuse him of throwing his life away, of wasting so much potential. The only way such a move would be sensible would be if Jesus was right – that this man would indeed have great riches in heaven. This man lacked such faith; only in hindsight do we see that he chose poorly, that his riches have now been lost when they could have been eternal.

Do we have such faith today? Can we be contented with Christ alone? The encouragement that we have as we serve among the poor is the profound joy we meet within our friends who live in such miserable conditions. The poor in Christ are perhaps the happiest people on earth.

4.   Mission in the Way of Christ

In Jesus, we see the deepest and purest self-revelation of God. If we want to know what God is like, we see it in Jesus, "the image of the invisible God" (Col. 1:15). And He was among us, there to touch and to converse with, true flesh and blood He ate, drank, walked and slept – and bled and died. We also found our own destiny to be re-made in His image and to reveal what God is like through Christ's presence in us.

It becomes clear that the practice of being with the poor is applicable to all of His disciples. We remember the marginalized, the oppressed, the excluded, not only because they are one among the many sociological groups that make up humanity, but because God in Christ made it a priority to bring good news to the poor and deliverance to the oppressed.

> "The Spirit of the Lord is upon me, for he has appointed me to preach Good News to the poor. He has sent me to proclaim that captives will be released, that the blind will see, that the downtrodden will be freed from their oppressors, and that the time of the Lord's favor has come." (Luke 4:18-19 NIV).

Through the poor, our sins against one another are most clearly revealed. And when sin is revealed, God calls us to receive correction, confess our sin, and turn and receive His mercy and follow Him on the way of righteousness.

Crisis Evangelism

Historically, crisis is a period in nation or world affairs determinative of the future, for fruition or ruin.

Economically, crisis is the breaking point of industry and business from which prosperity will return or collapse will occur.

Dramatically, crisis is the event toward which the play has moved and from which it will precede to its consummation.

Biblically, crisis is the stage reached when divine intervention is justified in order to prevent further disaster.

Etymologically and theologically, crisis means judgment. The noun derived from the Greek verb "krinein" to judge, from which we get such words as "Critic, Critical, and Criticism". A crisis represents a judgment, divine or human on the behaviour of men and nations, whether worthy or unworthy.

TYPES OF CRISIS

Life seems happy and beautiful when everything is going as planned. But what happens when crisis strikes? Are you prepared to face tough crisis situations that we all may face at one point in our lives or another? There are 5 types of crisis situations that you should think about and be prepared for.

1.   Death of a loved one:

The death of a loved one is a type of crisis situation that is literally beyond your control. We often take the presence and support of loved ones in our life for granted, only to be left heartbroken and shattered when they pass away.

2.   Bankruptcy

If multi-billion naira companies can turn bankrupt overnight, we are common men. Bankruptcy is a crisis of life that you can indeed be well prepared for. Keep aside a fixed amount of money every month as savings that you can access only in terrible emergencies. This piggy bank will help you sail through bankruptcy, a terrible type of crisis that it is.

3. Unexpected Failure

No matter how hard you try, and plan and how hard you focus on your efforts, failure is a part and parcel of business and professional life. Prepare for this type of crisis by mentally accepting the fact that you will fall down on your path to success.

4.   Breakup of a relationship

The breakup of a relationship can be one of the most disastrous emotional crises of life. Whether it is a parent-child, husband-wife or a girlfriend-boyfriend relationship, a breakup causes emotional trauma (Shock) and psychological stress that can affect the mental stability of the best of us.

5.   Loss of good health

You may be in good health right now, but have you ever wondered what life would be like if you lose one of your vital senses? Loss of good health is a type of crisis in life that we all must accept, and be prepared for.

This book comes in a time where there are many unrest or crises in all part of the world. Christians are expected to conduct themselves very well and use this opportunity to lead unbelievers to Christ.

It's difficult to evangelize when someone is almost losing hope. How do we find hope when hope is lost? The Bible says: The Lord is close to the brokenhearted; he rescues those whose spirits are crushed Psalms 34:18.

Crises evangelism is not the duty of everybody but a duty of Christians who have accepted to do the will of the Lord. Evangelism, mission work, and leading unbelievers to Christ during crisis should be done by genuine Christian.

Looking at the ministry today, many missionaries, Pastors, evangelists etc disorganized the work of evangelism and mission instead of leading unbelievers to Christ; they are busy leading believers to the world of Satan.

You must be selected by God not by man or the advice of your pastor nor your wife or friends etc. If you are selected by God you will not be afraid or lack word to say during these confused situations.

Note your appointment is "divine" not from human or any authority. The Lord said to Jeremiah: "I appoint you to stand up against nations and kingdoms…" (Jeremiah 1:10 NLT)

Mind you, no one has the power to appoint you to stand against nations and kingdoms except the Lord of Host. This means you need not to be afraid of anybody. Once you discover that your appointment and power is unlimited and supernatural (is from God) you will do beyond expectation. During crisis people need encouragements, future hope and someone who will comfort them. At this time, your encouragements should be pointed to Christ the Ultimate hope for everyone, what they need is hope in Christ Jesus; tell them about Jesus who knows about their situations and the calamity they found themselves in. Try and let them know that God is not happy about their situation and if they come to Jesus they will find rest. Jesus said:

"Come to me, all you who are weary and burdened, and I will give you rest" (Matt 11:28 NIV)

Make sure they know that the enemy (devil) is happy about their situation. Jesus said: The thief does not come except to steal, and to kill, and to destroy. I have come that they may have life, and that they may have it more abundantly" (John 10:10 NKJV)
Today we have well know crisis which is known as "religious crisis" where one religion is fighting the other which is one of the major concern in the world today; many people have lose their lives through this crisis which many of them are looking for where they will find rest. Your duty is to direct them to Christ, the Ultimate giver of peace and rest. NOTE, that God had called you for this task. You should always look for opportunity to talk to them about Christ (remember incarnational mission). When your dream dies, God has a new dream waiting for you. A new path. A new journey. Maybe a new ministry or message. A new passion. Whatever your loss, God can take your pain and do something new in you and through you. I know this is theory, but by the time you will apply it practically, always seek and wait for God to tell you what to do and how to start.

CHAPTER **5** NON-VERBAL APPROACHES OF MISSION

Living an exemplary life

Christians should know that many people both Christians and unbelievers watch them to learn many things from. Today people are tired of listening to preaching and teachings, they want to see what you are preaching and teaching in your life.

Your dressing:

The clothing worn in Biblical times was very different from what we wear today. Both men and women wore a loose, woolen, robe-like cloak or mantle as an outer garment. It was fastened at the waist with a belt or sash. Many so-called Christian dress carelessly forgetting their body is God's temple (1 Cor 3:16). Since our body is God's temple, His temple must be dressed appropriately to His standards. Your dressing should be decent as you represent Christ your Master.

The Oxford advance learners Dictionary define "Dress" as a piece of women's clothing that is made in one piece and cover the body down to legs, sometimes reaching to below the knees. Same dictionary defines "dress" as clothes for either men or women to wear.

Dressing

Men's Dressing

A Christian must dress in a manner that reveals or manifests God to the world and in a manner that does not make a sin. But if a Christian accepts the world, dresses like the world, what is the difference between such a Christian and the world?

> You are the salt of the earth. But if the salt loses its saltiness, how can it be made salty again? It is no longer good for anything, except to be thrown out and trampled underfoot (Mt. 5:13 NIV)

Men's body parts are private and they sexually entice females thus they must be decently dressed. Modesty is an attitude of the heart (1 Timothy 3:2) as well as a manner of dress. Modesty considers how we think about ourselves in relation to God, which is reflected in the way we dress.

Women's dressing

> And I want women to be modest in their appearance. They should wear decent and appropriate clothing and not draw attention to themselves by the way they fix their hair or by wearing gold or pearls or expensive clothes (1 Timothy 2:9 NLT).

Christians are expected to be role model in the society. As a Christian, we need to dress well to portray Christ in us. It is unfortunate today that one finds young girls and married women dressing indecently which attract male's attention.

The scripture says:"Women are not to wear men's clothing, and men are not wear women's clothing; the LORD your

G O D hate people who do such things."(Deuteronomy 22:5)G N V

Research shows that those who wear clothes of opposite sex some claim that they are worshipers of the goddess Astarte; sometimes their worship allowed women to wear men's clothing and men vice versa. But the question is, why did God create us male and female? Many people feel as if they are the one who created themselves. If we are to invite the worshipers of goddess Astarte to judge today's young men and women's dressing, they may probably say that, if they dress the way young men and women dressed, Astarte will not accept their worship because these dressing look Satanic.

Our young Christian girls involve themselves in wearing trousers which is Biblically condemned. God creates us male and female and we are expected to honour the difference. How do you expect an unbeliever in the village who in their village and culture condemn or discourage men or women who wear opposite sex clothing, to welcome you with your evangelism team that wear dress of opposite sexes? Will it be possible for the team to win souls for Christ? There was a story of an evangelism team that went to a remote village, with some of the girls wear trousers. As they arrived, they visited the village head; at their arrival, they introduced themselves to the village head. After the introduction, the village head responded that; "it is a taboo in our culture for a woman to wear trouser, please I do not permit you to enter my village because you may corrupt the society, kindly go back and dress well".

The group went there to preach the gospel of our Lord Jesus Christ to the villagers; unfortunately the village head preach to them about decent dressing, and they went back home shamefully.

Most of the cultures and religions do not support women or men wearing dress that expose part of the body. Where then did we get this from? One may ask. Many women loss their husbands into the hands of young girls who wear dresses that expose their body. In-fact some men testify that when they see women with such kind of dresses, it makes them to arose emotionally and this increases high number of rape and adultery in the society.

(1 Timothy 2:9).

Clothing from an Islamic Perspective

Muslims are required to pay attention to their appearance, making sure that their clothing is beautiful and clean, especially when dealing with others and when performing the prayers, as the Qur'an states, "Children of Adam, wear your best clothes to every mosque." (Soorat Al-A'raaf, 7:31)

Islamic religion indicates that Clothing Serves a Number of Purposes

1. It covers the parts of the body which must be covered in public, following the standards of modesty which are innate

in all human beings: "Children of Adam, We have sent down clothing to you to conceal your private parts." (Soorat Al-A'raaf, 7:31)

2. It covers the body against heat, cold and harm in general. Heat and cold are weather phenomena which can harm people. Describing the benefits of clothing which He has provided for His servants, Allah states, "He has made shelters for you in the mountains and He has made garments for you to protect you from the heat and garments to protect you from each other's violence. In that way He perfects His blessing on you so that hopefully you may devote yourselves to Him." (Soorat An-Nahl, 16:81)

Forbidden Types of Clothing

1. Clothing that reveals the private parts: Muslims are required to cover their private parts with appropriate clothing, as the Qur'an states, "Children of Adam! We have sent down clothing to you to conceal your private parts." (Soorat Al-A'raaf, 7:26) Islam has fixed the standards of modesty for both men and women. For men, the minimum amount to be covered is between the navel and the knee. For women who are in the presence of men not related to them, they must cover their bodies except for their face and hands. Islam requires that clothing must also be loose enough to cover the body properly. Therefore, skin-tight

and see-through clothes are not allowed in Islam. In fact, the Prophet ﷺ warned those people who do not observe modesty in dress, calling them "types among the people of Hellfire", one of them being "women who are clothed yet naked".

2. Clothing that involves dressing like or imitating the opposite sex: This type of clothing is strictly forbidden in Islam and wearing it is considered one of the major sins. This imitation may be extended to include imitation in the manner of speaking, gait and movement, for Allah's Messenger ﷺ cursed men who wear women's clothes and women who wear men's clothes. (Sunan Abu Daawood: 4098) He also cursed men who make themselves look like women and women who make themselves look like men. (Saheeh Al-Bukhaaree: 5546) By directing men and women to observe different modes of dress, Islam takes into account the biological differences between them and encourages them to act in accordance with the dictates of reason and dictates of sound reason and the pure inner nature innate in all humans (fitrah).

3. Silk clothing or clothing adorned with gold or silk for men: Referring to gold and silk once, the Prophet ﷺ said, "These are forbidden for men among my followers but permissible for women." (Sunan Ibn Maajah: 3595; Sunan

Abu Daawood: 4057). By silk is meant pure silk obtained from the cocoon of the silkworm.

4. Extravagant clothing: The Prophet ﷺ once said, "Eat, give charity and wear clothes. Let no extravagance or pride be mixed with what you do." (Sunan An-Nasaa'ee: 2559). The manner of dressing, however, varies from one person to another depending on one's social position. If a person is rich, he may purchase clothing that a poor person cannot afford, given his monthly income, economic position and other financial obligations he has to fulfil. While a piece of clothing may be considered a form of extravagance for a poor person, it may not be considered as such for a rich person.

Today our young boys become the city cleaners, they wear trouser downward to their bottom which shows their boxers or pant. One day I stopped a taxi, I was going to Terminus market in Jos Plateau state, Nigeria. I enter the taxi 20meters further a young boy stopped the taxi when the driver stopped (a woman driver), she discovered that the boy's trouser wanted to fall, the women said, hey! "Your trouser will fall", but the boy reply "no it would not" she ask him "can't you see that you are about to display your penis"? The young boy answered, "that's how I dressed" and she said to him, "I cannot carry you in my car" because your dressing was indecent.

Many married men and women are doing worse than those of the young children and you can't lead someone to Christ if you are not connected to Christ!

Deu.22:5 clearly explain to us that God hates those who wear opposite sex clothing. The questions here are, "as a Christian, who are you worshiping with trouser or low-west? Is it God or goddess Astarte? If God hates you and your dressing why are you wasting your time in the Church?" And if you are Astarte worshiper, I don't think goddess Astarte will like to be watching you bottom every day. If you say you are preaching and worshiping God and God hates your act of dressing do you think He will crown your effort with success? Many so-call Christians say they don't know why people are not changing despite the television, radio and Sunday messages e.t.c. But I will like every believer or church gower to search his/herself; had it been all people are like you will there be any change at all? You cannot lead unbeliever to Christ, if you cannot change from bad ways. Make sure that you are a true believer you are in good relationship with God first, then you think of leading unbelievers to Christ. Jesus says a blind cannot lead a blind; they may all fall into a pit.

The Bible says:

"You should also know this, Timothy, that in the last days there will be very difficult times. For people will love only themselves and their money. They will be boastful and proud, scoffing at God, disobedient to their parents, and ungrateful. They will consider nothing sacred. They will be unloving and unforgiving; they will slander others and have no self-control; they will be cruel and have no interest in what is good. They will betray their friends, be reckless, be puffed up with pride, and love pleasure rather than God. They will act as if they are religious, but they will reject the power that could make them godly. You must stay away from people like that. They are the kind who work their way into people's homes and win the confidence of vulnerable women who are burdened with the guilt of sin and controlled by many desires"(2 Tim 3:1-6 NLT)

My beloved readers, the truth is that we are now in a modern world where almost everybody know how to read the Holy Bible. **BIBLE IS THE BASIC OF HUMAN MATURITY.** Do not allow any body to come with his or her false teaching because he or she wants to enrich his or herself. Looking at the above scripture, you will agree with me that, there are many road side churches today who are careless about your dressing. They quote the Bible wrongly saying that the Bible say 'God is not after our physical appearance but our heart'; let me tell you, it is good to study your Bible very well. Your Bible is not different from mine, don't allow this new generation churches to take you away from the love of God. I don't know your church, but my point here is that if you find yourself in this type of churches, I don't ask you to change your church but do exactly what the Bible wants you to do because church will not take you to heaven. If you truly pray and study your Bible, and asking God to aid you to abide by His word, he will surely help you and tell you what to do.

Don't forget the Oxford Dictionary's definition of "dress"; is clothing that covered once knees downward. If world expects you to cover your body well and even from your knees downward; then there is no reason why the child of God will go to church with short trouser or mini-Skirt; a skirt that exposes your private parts to people. The dictionary definition is secular, if the secular world expects decency dressing, God expect more. Many people are perishing in their sins because of resistance to change, they need someone to help them; don't allow your way of life tarnish the work of God on earth. If you are beautiful, use your beauty for the Gospel, if you are a musician use your voice to glorify the name of God, so that when the Lord comes, you will receive the crow of glory from your creator.

Interacting with people

Interaction is a medium of communicating with people. Someone who is leading unbelievers to Christ needs to communicate with enthusiasm. The following areas shall be discussed to enable us interact well as followers of Christ.

Family:

When I was single, I studied the life of some families and I discovered that the church mission had started failing in some of our Christian homes which lead some of the family members to deny their faith in Christ.

As parents, you should know that it's your responsibility to make sure that your home is happy, and provide enough food and shelter; it is your duty to make sure that all member of the family participate in bible studies and other church activities. The unfortunate thing that normally happens in Christian homes is that most parents do not know that they are the pastor of their homes. Even if you are a pastor or member, do you know that the children you have or will give birth to are not yet Christians? Until they confess with their mouth and accept Christ as their personal Lord and Saviour. Do you know that if you fell to bring up your children in a Godly way God will ask you why?

Proverb 22:6 says:

> "Train a child in the way he should go, and when he is old he will not turn from it (NIV)

Do you know that it is your duty as a parent to make sure that your family makes heaven?

The most disappointed of all in some of our Christian families, is that we don't train our children where to go and how they should leave their live. Parents should observe the movement of their children, make sure they study the bible in their day to day activities, and monitor the kind of friends they have so that they cannot corrupt their minds.

As parents you should know that your family is your first mission field. Many parents don't care about which kind of dress their children should have. As a parent you need to encourage your children to learn how to make decent dressing so that it will not be a barrier to the entire Christendom

My late father, Rev. Dauda Madaki ever said, **"if you want to know the type of a pastor in a particular church, check the life style of his members"**. It means good tress bear good fruits. You can't have a church without a family, this means if parents are mission mandate, their children will be mission mandate, and if they are money mandate, their children will have the same desire even more than theirs. As a believer, your families need to leave peacefully and your moral acts will attract the attention of unbelievers, when they see your family is living in peace; they will love to ask you the secret. Now, this is the opportunity you are waiting for. You should change your discussion to spiritual matter. Example of changing discussion to spiritual discussion is found in Acts 1:6-8

> "So when they had come together, they ask him, "Lord, will you at this time restore the kingdom to Israel?" he said to them, it is not for you to know time or seasons that the father has fixed by his own authority but you will receive power when the holy spirit come upon you, and you will be may witnesses in Jerusalem and in all   Judea and Samaria, and to the end of the earth (ESV)

> Jesus remained focus and he tried to remind his disciples to

know that he came to this sinful world for a purpose and they shall remain on that purpose (to carry out gospel to all nations from Jerusalem, Judea, and Samaria, and the end of the earth).

Try to look for opportunity like this and use Jesus' methodology prayerfully so that the unbeliever will get to know Christ through your peaceful, loving and caring family. Mind you Jesus reminded His disciples their starting point; and don't forget that your starting point is Jerusalem which is your family. Let' your interaction with your family be Godly, peaceful, caring and loving because there are many unbelievers outside your family watching to see if there is something good from Christian homes, and if you are living in the same area with unbelievers, and they find you are fighting with your wife and children after Sunday services, your children are dressing indecently, sleeping with ladies and men outside your house; then what impact is your family making to unbelieving society around you?

That is why Paul warns timothy that: "Let no one despise you for your youth, but set the believers an example in speech, in conduct, in love, in faith, in purity". (1timothy 4:12) ESV

In this case you should know that your goal is to set an example to your family, community, market, office and everywhere you may have find yourself; in speech, in conduct, in love, in faith and in purity this should be and continue to be your great priority.

Office:

Christians must do their work differently from that of the world's point of view Paul says: "Be very careful, then, how live-not as unwise but as wise, making the most of every opportunity, because the days are evil. Therefore do not be foolish, but understand what the lord's will is". (Eph. 5:15-16) NIV.

Many Christian fail to understand that their office is a mission field; most of the time, they use their office to cheat, embezzle money and deny people of their right. Christians should know that it is expected of them to walk differently from that of the world. In government offices, tertiary institutions such as University, Polytechnic, and other colleges, banking and financial houses, law firms, arm forces etc you will discover that, corruption has reach up to a chronic stage that only prayers and God intervention will save us from this situation. Have you ever asked yourself why God makes you a professional in the area of your specialization? Have you asked yourself why you have an officer? Mind you God gives you that profession to glory his name. And if God finds out that you are not helping people or using your office as it is expected He will make you to live that office then someone takes over.

Revelation 3:2-4 says:

> "Wake up, and strengthen what remains and is
> about to die, for I have not found your work
> complete in the sight of my God. Remember, then,

what you received and heard. Keep it and repent. If you will not wake up, I will come like a thief, and you will not know at what hour I will come against you" (ESV).

Be wise and make use of every opportunity you have, because the days are evil. Don't agree with this saying "If you cannot beat them join them" this saying is demonic once you begin to think about the saying and the caliber of people in your organization/ministry, the next thought that will come to you is LET ME JOIN THEM. Note that God has given you the privilege to serve in your organization not because you are the most educated or talented than others but it is His grace. As a believer, once you see things are moving the way that is not expected, start thinking on how you will put those things in order.

Many Christians see politics as a dirty work. It is not a dirty work; rather the people who do the politics are dirty. If a Politician will use his office to reach out unbelievers, believe me he or she will get more believers than the pastors or evangelist because people come to them every day either willingly or unwillingly and this politician know how to convince people, though it demands God's intervention

There are many offices and profession, but what is required from you is to be determine to do the work for Christ; don't forget Jesus' methodology of ministry (changing your discussion to spiritual discussion). The bible says:

❋
44

Who is wise and understanding among you? Let him show it by his good life, by deeds done in the humility that comes from wisdom. But if you harbor bitter envy and selfish ambition in your hearts, do not boast about it or deny the truth. Such "wisdom" does not come down from heaven but is earthly, unspiritual, of the devil. For where you have envy and selfish ambition, there you find disorder and every evil practice. But the wisdom that comes from heaven is first of all pure; then peace-loving, considerate, submissive, full of mercy and good fruit, impartial and sincere. Peacemakers who sow in peace raise a harvest of righteousness. (James 3:13-18 NIV).

Market:

Market is a regular gathering of people for the purchase and sale of provisions, livestock, and other commodities. Unfortunately, people use market to cheat customers and they also use the name of God in other to convince their customers to buy or pay for fake goods and services from them. Moreover, as a lay person if you go to the market it's very difficult to know which product is a genuine from the seller. During Jesus' ministry on earth, He used market as a medium to minister to people. Jesus said:

"Give, and it will be given to you. A good measure, pressed down, shaken together and running over, will be poured into your lap. For with the measure you use, it will be measured to you." (Luke 6:38 NIV).

Unfortunately, if you go to the market you find out that the measure used for buying from you is different from the one they will used to sell. Christians who are expected to be people of respect, high integrity and competent, are now the great "419s" in the market. Today many people prefer to buy something from a Muslim or unbelieving brother, they prefer to buy or pay for goods and services than from Christian Brother. As Christians, we are expected to use the medium we have in the market to reach the unbelievers; use a good measure, sale good products and interact with your customers very well, through that, unbelieving customers will trust you and through the leadership of the Holy Spirit, the Holy Spirit will help you to lead them to Christ.

Generosity:

Being generous begins with treating each person as though they have already achieved the potential for greatness that is in every one of us. It is in essence a sincere desire to make others' live easier or more pleasant.

Being generous as Christians should not be over emphasized; Jesus our role model was generous to known and unknown people, He was generous to believers and unbelievers. In-fact, as for Jesus he did not come for the righteous, rather for the unrighteous to be saved. But go and learn what this means: 'I desire mercy, not sacrifice.' For I have not come to call the righteous, but sinners." (Matt 9:13 NIV)

If Jesus whom we claim to be His followers love sinners, came for sinners, healed sinners, chatted with sinners, ate with sinners, provided food for sinners and died for sinners; then why can't we as Christ body be generous to people? Many follow Jesus because of His generosity, why can't you be generous so that unbelievers will come to Christ through you? Do you remember this story where Jesus told a rich Jew to be generous?

> Now a man came up to Jesus and asked, "Teacher, what good thing must I do to get eternal life?" "Why do you ask me about what is good?" Jesus replied. "There is only one who is good. If you want to enter life, obey the commandments." "Which ones?" the man inquired. Jesus replied, "'Do not murder, do not commit adultery, do not steal, do not give false testimony, honor your father and mother,' and 'love your neighbor as yourself.'" "All these I have kept," the young man said. "What do I still lack?" Jesus answered, "If you want to be perfect, go, sell your possessions and give to the poor, and you will have treasure in heaven. Then come, follow me." When the young man heard this, he went away sad, because he had great wealth. Then Jesus said to his disciples, "I tell you the truth, it is hard for a rich man to enter the kingdom of heaven. Again I tell you, it is easier for a camel to go through the eye of a needle

than for a rich man to enter the kingdom of God."
Matt 19:16-24 NIV

Many Christians today are like the young wealthy Jew who is very stingy; he does not want to share his wealth with the poor and doesn't want the poor to be financially free. This is now the common and serious problem affecting the Christian community. The secret of having more wealth is "sharing;" do you also remember the story of Jesus and the young boy with two fish and five loaves of bread?

> That evening the disciples came to him and said, "This is a desolate place, and it is getting late. Send the crowds away so they can go to the villages and buy food for themselves." But Jesus replied, "That isn't necessary — you feed them." "Impossible!" they exclaimed. "We have only five loaves of bread and two fish!" "Bring them here," he said. Then he told the people to sit down on the grass. And he took the five loaves and two fish, looked up toward heaven, and asked God's blessing on the food. Breaking the loaves into pieces, he gave some of the bread and fish to each disciple, and the disciples gave them to the people. They all ate as much as they wanted, and they picked up twelve baskets of leftovers. About five thousand men had eaten from those five loaves, in addition to all the women and children! (Matt 14:15-21 NLT)

Had it been the boy kept the bread for himself it may not be enough for him and his family; but because the boy was generous with the small, the small quantity of food fed about five thousand men. Women and children are excluded from the counting and have about twelve full basket returns; what a wonderful character of generosity. The story of Lazarus and the rich Man in Luke 16:19-31 reminds us that anyone who do good will receive the reward of being good on earth and in heaven; learn to be generous and you will never go to your creator empty handed.

Food for thought

- Generosity can also be forgiving a person's shortcomings or mistakes.

- Don't push yourself on being generous; just try to summon it as instinct tells you to.

- Generosity should come from heart not because you want to make a name.
    Try to avoid being generous on cash, as it can cause some issues between you and others. If someone you know asks for it, consider the following: Are they going to pay it back? What will the money be used for? If you like the answers, then go on, but remember, don't give out your entire bank account, and try to find something in the deal for you - a return on your investment if you like.

6

STRATEGIES OF MISSION WORK

Be Prayerful

I wander how people don't know the value of prayer. Do you know that in every town and city there are evil forces in every four angle of the city? The only weapon to fight these forces of darkness is prayers.

What is Prayer?

There are four Hebrew terms prayers are rendered:

1.   Tepilla, in general, supplication to God (Ps 65:2; 80:4; Isa 1:15; Job 16:17; etc.); also intercession, supplication for another (2 Kings 19:4; Isa 37:4; Jer 7:16; 11:14).

2.   Palal, to "judge," and then "to interpose as umpire, mediator" (Gen 20:7; Deut 9:20; 1 Sam 7:5; Job 42:8), with the general sense of prayer (Ps 5:2; 1 Sam 1:26; 2 Sam 7:27; etc.).

3.   `Atar, "to burn incense," therefore to pray to God (Job 33:26), the prayers of the righteous being likened to incense (Rev 5:8).

4.   Lahash, to "whisper a prayer" uttered in a low voice (Isa 26:16). Lahash is a quiet whispering prayer (like the whispering forms of incantation in 3:3); sorrow renders speechless in the long run; and a consciousness of sin

crushes so completely that a man does not dare to address God aloud (cf. 29:4).

Prayer may be defined as a direct communication between man and his creator, to request for something or for someone or to seek for forgiveness or render appreciation.

Because God is personal, all people can offer prayers to him. However, sinners who have not trusted their lives to Jesus Christ for their salvation remain separated from God. So, unbelievers may pray, but their payer does not have the basis for a rewarding fellowship with God. Christians recognize their dependence upon their Creator. They have every reason to express gratitude for God's blessings. But they have far more reason to respond to God than this.

Let's see some ways we are expected to pray to God Almighty.

1.	Faith: The most meaningful prayer comes from a heart that places its trust in God who has acted and spoken in Jesus history and the teachings of the Bible. God speaks to us through the Bible, and we in turn speak to Him in trustful, believing prayer. Assured by the Scripture that God is personal, living, active, all-knowing, all-wise, and all-powerful, we know that God can hear and help us.

2.	Worship: In worship we recognize what is of highest worth-not ourselves, others, or our work, but God. Only the highest divine being deserves our highest respect. Guided by Scripture, we set our values in accord with God's will and perfect standards. Before God, angels hide their faces and cry, "Holy, holy, holy is the Lord of hosts" (Isa 6:3).

3. Confession: Awareness of God's holiness leads to consciousness of our own sinfulness. Like the prophet Isaiah, we exclaim, "Woe is me, for I am undone! Because I am a man of unclean lips, and I dwell in the midst of a people of unclean lips; for my eyes have seen the King, the Lord of hosts" (Isa 6:5). By sinning we hurt ourselves and those closest to us; but first of all and worst of all, sin is against God (Ps 51:4). We must confess our sins to God to get right with Him. We need not confess them to another being. But we should confess them directly to God, who promises to forgive us of all our unrighteousness (1 John 1:9). Note: if you hurt or make someone angry, you need to make peace with that person.

4. Adoration: God is love, and He has demonstrated His love in the gift of His Son. The greatest desire of God is that we love Him with our whole being (Matt 22:37). Our love should be expressed, as His has been expressed, in both deeds and words. People sometimes find it difficult to say to others and to God, "I love you." But when love for God fills our lives, we will express our love in prayer to the one who

is ultimately responsible for all that we are.

5. Praise: The natural outgrowth of faith, worship, confession, and adoration is praise. We speak well of one whom we highly esteem and love. The one whom we respect and love above all others nature receives our highest commendation. We praise Him for His mighty acts "Praise Him for His mighty deeds; Praise Him according to His excellent greatness!" (Ps 150:2 NASU), and for His "righteous judgments" (Ps 119:164). For God Himself, for His works, and for His words, His people give sincere praise.

6. Thanksgiving: we are unthankful because we think we have not received what we deserve? But if we got what we "deserved," we would be condemned because of our guilt. As sinners, we are not people of God by nature. We have no claim upon His mercy or grace. Nevertheless, He has forgiven our sins, granted us acceptance as His people, and given us His righteous standing and a new heart and life. Ingratitude marks the ungodly (Rom 1:21). Believers, in contrast, live thankfully. God has been at work on our behalf in countless ways. So in everything, even for the discipline that is unpleasant, we give thanks (Col 3:17; 1 Thess. 5:18).

7. Dedicated Action: Christ's example does not require us to withdraw from society, but to render service to the needy

in a spirit of prayer. He wept over Jerusalem in compassionate prayer, and then He went into the city to give His life a ransom for many. Authentic prayer will be the source of courage and productivity, as it was for the prophets and apostles.

8.   Request: Prayer is not only response to God's grace as brought to us in the life and work of Jesus and the teaching of Scripture; it is also a request for our needs and the needs of others.

Looking at the above eight listed ways of prayer, Christians are expected to always pray for unbelievers. Mission and evangelism is not only a monthly or weekly duty rather it should be a continual programme for the church and individual. People are always selfish during their prayer; they always think goodies for themselves and invite calamity for their enemies. Jesus said:

> "You have heard that it was said, 'Love your neighbor and hate your enemy.' But I tell you: Love your enemies and pray for those who persecute you, that you may be sons of your Father in heaven. He causes his sun to rise on the evil and the good, and sends rain on the righteous and the unrighteous" If you love those who love you, what reward will you get? Are not even the tax collectors doing that? (Matt 5:43-46 NIV).

Their was a pastor who gave a story while preaching in the church, he said: there was a young man who went to a restaurant to buy food; he started eating without prayer. The person sitting close to him asked him, "are you a Christian?" The young man answer "Yes", the person asked again "are you a dog?" The young man said "No", he said to the young man it's only dogs eats food without prayers.

This story makes me to understand that there are Christian who are dogs in behaviour, even though they are human and claim to be Christians, they go to church every Sunday for worship, but they don't know the value of prayers in their Christian Life. No wander Jesus said to a Canaanite woman: It is not good to take the children's bread and throw it to the little dogs." (Matt 15:26 NKJV)

Tokumboh Adeyemo describes Jesus' Answer "dogs" "as a Jewish term of abuse for gentiles". But the use of this term by Jesus was seeing beyond the woman and the disciples understanding. By the way, who are Canaanites? It is the biblical name for ancient Palestine west of the Jordan River, the promise land of the Israelites, who conquered and occupied it during the later part of the 2nd millennium B.C. probably, this woman was part of the remnant of the ancient Palestine who followed the Israelites to promise land. These people may be seen as unbelievers (non-Jews).

The man who calls this young man a dog was not wrong to nickname this man dog because in the Christian setting, if one is born from a Christian family, it does not guarantee and qualify the person to be a genuine Christian. The response of this Canaanite woman to Jesus is of interest: "Yes, Lord, Yet even the dogs eat the crumbs that fall from their master table" (Matthew 15:27 ESV).

Her response shows that the children and the dogs have same master, but what distinct both of them, is their identity (the children are human while the dogs are master's animals). Christians are expected to pray for those who are trying day-in-day-out to see they lead unbelievers to Christ, they should pray for themselves, their family, their leaders and many others. We should know that we are created by one God "as the dog and children are having the same master" our duty as Christians is to look for alternative as we are praying to God to help us change them from darkness to light.

Leading on unbeliever to Christ is declaring an open battle with the devil (Satan). That's why Paul encouraged the Ephesians to "be strong in the Lord and in the strength of His might" (Eph. 6:10 E.S.V). Paul concludes his speech by reminding the believers that they engage in a war and need God's power and amour to protect themselves. The source of their power is God, whose mighty power will enable them to resist the enemy (Satan).

Christian should know that a prayer-less Christian is "a power-less Christian" (true life story) there was a man who was sleeping at night, he wake up and saw someone's shadow in his room, the man stood up and he saw the shadow was moving in the room; the room owner shouted "in Jesus name" the shadow answered "Amen". Now who is the owner of the room among them? Is it the enemy or the person who resist the devil? Looking at this story, one will discover that this Christian is a power less Christian. He can't use the name of Jesus to resist the devil; through serious prayers, knowing the truth the power of his resurrection will give you the power to stand against powers and principalities in the heavily places.

As you embark and continue into the mission of reconciliation, you should know that God has also provided the full amour that you need. But before you use these amours effectively, be encouraged to put it on and do the following:

1.   Remind yourself every day of the generosity you need to show not just to feel.

2.   When interacting with others, notice the things you could do to make their lives easier or happier.

3.   Think of specific ways you can be good to known and un-known people.

4.   Extend this thoughtfulness to strangers, even if all you do is smile and say hello, or let them on to the highway in front of you.

5.   Think about how your action will them impact them,

6.   As you're consciously generous to others, it will get easier and easier. Soon the time will come when you're

automatically generous. The natural progression is that others will be more generous to you. After all, it's true that "what goes around comes around."

7.   Remember that generosity is not just a decision, it's a lifestyle.

CHAPTER 7
RECOGNISING THE PLAN OF GOD
See them the way god sees them

Jesus whom handed over the ministry of reconciliation saw unbelievers the way God sees them. How can a Christian see unbelievers the way God see them? He must see them as sheeps without a shepherd and have compassion on them. Some preachers, evangelist and missionaries join this gospel ministry in order to make money, some to destroy other ministers' labour and to others God call them to lead unbelievers to Christ. A person that is out to make money never see unbelievers the way God sees them. God saw them weary and scattered, like a sheep having no shepherd. Christians must be people filled with God's compassion, love and care for the lost ones.

Unfortunately Christianity has become a thing to show who is who, who is educated, who can speak well or who can speak in tongues, who is rich etc. the concept of Christianity today is different from that of the early church perspective. The question here is what happens during the early church fathers? Acts 4:32-34 says:

> "All the believers were one in heart and mind. No one claimed that any of his possessions was his own, but they shared everything they had. With great power the apostles continued to testify to the

resurrection of the Lord Jesus, and much grace was upon them all. There were no needy persons among them. For from time to time those who owned lands or houses sold them, brought the money from the sales and put it at the apostles' feet, and it was distributed to anyone as he had need". NIV

The early church keep on growing day by day because they have love and compassion for the missing souls; they share everything they have with great Joy and there were no needy people among them.

The church today is trying to practice it, but find it difficult, because about 80-95% of the church members today are like Ananias and Sapphira (hypocrites). They don't have loving and caring heart; most of them are backbiters and malicious, that is why the church today is declining. A missionary once told me that today in the United State of America, Churches are being sold to business men and is being turned to Hotels, Bars for many ungodly purposes.

In the first 5 centuries, Christianity dominated countries where are now dominated by Islam. The problem with Christianity and its leaders is "ARGUMENTS". We should forget about all arguments and other un-necessary things and focus on mission (ministry of reconciliation). Why do Christians see unbelievers as their enemies? Why should they be seen as enemies? They should not be seen as enemies because any group of sheep that go out for grazing without a shepherd must destroy people's crops in their farm. If that is the case, it means one should not be angry of their actions whether positively or negatively because they live their lives without a teacher, mentor or guidance from the Holy Spirit.

Compassion

In many instances, compassion is the rendering of the Hebrew word elsewhere translated mercy. It is also the rendering of the Hebrew word "hamal" (to "be gentle, clement"; "concern" in the NIV), as in 1 Sam 23:21. In Ex 2:6 the rendering is "pity" and in 1 Sam 15:3,15; 2 Sam 21:7 it is rendered "spared," as in 2 Chron 36:15,17 where we read that God "had compassion on His people and on His dwelling place," i.e., He spared them. It is written that "the Lord is full of compassion" (James 5:11), and that "just as a father has compassion on his children, so the Lord has compassion on those who fear Him" (Ps 103:13).

If you are compassionate to someone status of living, it means you will be merciful to his or her behavioral acts, sinful acts and all what the person will do out of ignorant; that is why Jesus said this on the cross: "Father, forgive them, for they do not know what they are doing." (Luke 23:34 NIV)

Even at the point of death, Jesus still had compassion on those who killed him. It is unfortunate that Christians today live their lives without focus and direction, while the church seen unbelievers as enemies. God does not need weapons to protects you, what he needs from you is total submission and wait for His divine intervention.

Looking at the story of Moses and the Israelites in Egypt, the Israelites were oppressed, maltreated and killed by the Egyptians. The Bible did not tell us that the Israelites went out with weapons to fight the Egyptians, rather the cried unto the Lord for mercy. The question is "how many times have you genuinely cried to God for His divine mercy?" Note that a child that is not having good relationship with his father cannot ask him for help. A true Christian is someone who is filled with love, because our God is Love. A Christian must be someone who is compassionate because God has compassion over his children (John 3:16).

The love and compassion that God has for human race is different from the world's point of view. In Genesis chapter 3, man had fallen short from the glory of God almighty. God had compassion on man and does not want man to continue living without having good relationship with his creator. That's why Paul encourage the people of Corinthians that:

> All this is from God, who reconciled us to himself through Christ and gave us the ministry of reconciliation: that God was reconciling the world to himself in Christ, not counting men's sins against them. And he has committed to us the message of reconciliation. We are therefore Christ's ambassadors, as though God were making his appeal through us. We implore you on Christ's behalf: Be reconciled to God. God made him who had no sin to be sin for us, so that in him we might become the righteousness of God. 2 Cor 5:18-21 NIV

The church should know that they have great task ahead, reconciling men to God. Unfortunately the church today is busy counting their sin against them or themselves which was not the task given by the Lord Jesus Christ. The church should note that at the process of reconciling men to God, they will face trial and challenges. Dear reader, know that man had sinned against God in Genesis 3 and after the fall of man, man have ever return to God, but God came in human standard to save man from sin. God is expecting men to do likewise. Isaiah 49:8-9 says:

This is what the LORD says: "In the time of my favor I will answer you, and in the day of salvation I will help you; I will keep you and will make you to be a covenant for the people, to restore the land and to reassign its desolate inheritances, to say to the captives, 'Come out,' and to those in darkness, 'Be free!'. (NIV)
As God's fellow workers do not receive God's grace in vain, show compassion to others and be reconciled to God.

CHAPTER 8

UNVEILING THE WORD
Tell them about the good news

This is another important chapter of this book. There are many unbelievers that are supposed to be believers, but because of wrong method of presentation, they have rejected Christ completely. In all you do, always refer to where and how Jesus started His ministry on earth. Jesus is a good example to emulate. He did not only use one method in His ministry am not advising you to stick to one methods in different areas or villages you go for ministry, always think backward to Jesus' time and use the different method he used at the time His ministry. Before Jesus started His, ministry he engaged in forty days and forty nights of prayers and fasting. This made His ministry on earth very unique, powerful, miraculous, and successful. Many people today engage themselves in God's ministry without God's invitation and approval. The Old Testament prophets had to argue with God to be sure of their calling. The prophets like Jeremiah (Jeremiah 1:4-9), Ezekiel (Ezek. 2:1-3:15, Samuel (the Priest) 1Samuel 3:1-21) and many other great men of God are examples. In the New Testament, Paul (Soul) was called by God and his calling was confirmed by Ananias. All these people make great changes in the life of their present community and Christendom in general.

Matthew 28:19-20 has always been a difficult passage to explain. Some people are of the view that all are to go while some say only pastors, evangelist, elders, deacons and some other leaders. Jesus did not differentiate who to go and who to stay; however, in other not to contradict what was said earlier in this book, there are those who will go, those who will stay to pray and those who will support financially. The Bible says in Acts 4:32-37:

> ...For instance, there was Joseph, the one the apostles nicknamed Barnabas (which means "Son of Encouragement"). He was from the tribe of Levi and came from the island of Cyprus. He sold a field he owned and brought the money to the apostles for those in need. (NLT)

After Jesus was ascended to heaven, the disciples gathered in a group (church) waiting for the anointing of the Holy Spirit. Don't forget Jesus' instruction in Acts 1:8, Jesus gave His disciples their starting point Jerusalem (Home) before going to the parts of the world. Joseph (Barnabas) whose name and meaning was mentioned in Acts 4:36-37, during the apostles' time, had a financial supporting mechanism in the ministry. As said earlier, many do not know whether they were called to support or to minister. Many do not know whether they were called to perform miracles or to teach. God uses everyone in the ministry in different areas which allows people perform his or her duty according the ability given by God. At the early stage of the gospel, the apostles waited for the anointing of the Holy Spirit.

Unfortunately, many people today who claim to be called by God have their personal agenda apart from the one in Matthew 28:19-20. Note that any ministry agenda that is different from that of Matthew 28:19-20 is a counterfeit. Many of those who claimed to be called do not have time to study about what God called them to do. They are always in a hurry! If it takes Jesus three years to train and prepare his disciples for the ministry, there is no reason why many Christians will want to go for two or six months training to pastor a church or to be a missionary; that is why Christianity is declining today. At this time, it is important to outline some strategies that will help in witnessing Christ to unbelievers:

1.   All have Sinned: Romans 3:23-26 says:

> For all have sinned; all fall short of God's glorious standard. Yet now God in his gracious kindness declares us not guilty. He has done this through Christ Jesus, who has freed us by taking away our sins. For God sent Jesus to take the punishment for our sins and to satisfy God's anger against us. We are made right with God when we believe that Jesus shed his blood, sacrificing his life for us. God was being entirely fair and just when he did not punish those who sinned in former times. And he is entirely fair and just in this present time when he declares sinners to be right in his sight because they believe in Jesus (NLT).

Telling unbelievers about Christ is not a one day job. Some churches are engaging in soul wining (evangelism) once or twice a year, and claim they are fully engaged in the master's business. It is far more than that, is it possible for a parent to send a child to school, then come tomorrow or the next day with certificate? If the answer is no then it means the church today has failed. It also means that the church should not only engage on evangelism once or twice yearly but should send missionaries to stay there for five or six years. Remember the missionaries who came to this part of the world (Africa and Nigeria in Particular); they were not just coming once or twice only, but came to stay for months and years. They came to live with the people, teaching them until they understood. In doing that, some self ill others died while evangelizing. Those who intend to obey the Master's command should be ready to pay the price by accepting to be trained and for a reasonable numbers of years.

You cannot go to an unbeliever and tell him that "you are a sinner, accept Christ as his personal Lord and Saviour", before he or she believe you. You must take your time to stay with him or her, learn when and where to talk to him or her, show love and care to the unbeliever. You need to tell him or her about yours or other people's conversion, experience and tell them how you were once a sinner and how Jesus saved you.

2.   The wages of sin is Death: Romans 6:23 says: "For the wages of sin is death, but the gift of God is eternal life in Christ Jesus our Lord" (NIV).

If you did not explain very well to an unbeliever how you and others suffer in sin, (the first point), it may be very difficult for them to understand the second point. As a Christian you may have come across how you or someone's sin pays its wages to death. Anyone who lives in sin has no hope of eternity. The goodies of Romans 6:23 is the gift of eternal life. Many unbelievers today do not know anything about eternity; you who is leading them to Christ must explain everything to them. Note as pointed above in chapter two, "you should know what you believe and what they believe" this is very vital in leading unbelievers to Christ.

3.   Christ Died for You: Romans 5:8-11 (NLT):

> But God showed his great love for us by sending Christ to die for us while we were still sinners. And since we have been made right in God's sight by the blood of Christ, he will certainly save us from God's judgment. For since we were restored to friendship with God by the death of his Son while we were still his enemies, we will certainly be delivered from eternal punishment by his life. So now we can rejoice in our wonderful new relationship with God — all because of what our Lord Jesus Christ has done for us in making us friends of God.

The death and resurrection of Christ is the foundation of Christian faith. It is important to use every privilege you find yourself discussing with an unbeliever to lead them to Christ. Let them know that Christ came for our sin and die to rescue us from our sin. Explain the purpose of Christ coming and the benefit of His death.

4.   You Can Be Save: Ephesians 2:8-10 (NIV):

For it is by grace you have been saved, through faith-
and this not from yourselves, it is the gift of God- not
by works, so that no one can boast. For we are
God's workmanship, created in Christ Jesus to do
good works, which God prepared in advance for us
to do.

To God be the Glory, looking at the points 1, 2 and 3 they all
show your own and that of the unbeliever's limitation. The
unbeliever may be waiting for the solution or your directions. A sick
person cannot be healed, if the sickness is not discovered. Once the
unbeliever discovers his or her limitation, then you direct them to
take discussion on their limitation, to accept Christ as their
personal Lord and Saviour. Give them the assurance of life's
transformation from death to eternal life as it is in 2Corinthians
5:17.

5.   Lead them to Christ: Praise God!!! Once you reach this
stage you should have it in mind that God will take glory now or
latter. There are reason why the Word "later" is used because once
you have led them to Christ, some will send you away, because of
their religious background, some will behave as if they heard you
but not, some will ask you to give them time to think about it and
others may accept Christ as their personal Lord and Saviour. Don't
feel offended because they do not accept Christ. You are there to
do God's work; please allow God to do the finishing. Some of the
new converts we get during the once in a year evangelism may be

other missionaries labours and God is using you to do the finishing. Place it in your mind that, in every mission work, you may not be the person to do the finishing. If that is the case, allow God to do it Himself, or He will assign someone to do the finishing, the blessing shall be yours and God will receive the glory.

If God notice that after everything you are to take all His glory for yourself, He may not allow you to do the finishing so that you will not be filled with pride; do you remember Moses who took the Israelites out from Egypt? God might have discovered that if the Israelites discovered where Moses' body was buried, they may have been going there to worship his grave. This is because the Israelites sometimes forget God, and focus on Moses who was their Saviour (who brought them out of Egypt).

Once you start telling them about the Good News, it demands prayers and fasting. The mistake preachers normally make is they tell them that, they will not experience suffering, this is not true. Jesus said: "…anyone who wants to follow Him must carry His cross daily and follow him". cross means suffering, tribulations and persecution. That is why after they may have believed in Christ and latter experience suffering, tribulations and persecution they will prefer to go back, because that was not what they were told.

Moses told the Israelites that, God is taking them to a Land that is filled with milk and honey and when they came across the

Red Sea, they told him that you could have left us in Egypt.

Brethren, the way may seem rocky and difficult but definitely be assured that the end is going to be good. Don't think about the earthly end but your eternity.

CHAPTER

THE CHURCH OBLIGATION

The church and her responsibilities

Today's church is busy building mansions instead of mission. Many churches embarked on church maintenance project which is not the primary purpose of church ministry. Many pastors join the ministry without the passion of the work that is why today the church has lost its focus.

Rob Frost Says: "The church exits by mission in the same way that a fire exists by burning. It has been convincingly argued that mission is the hallmark of a genuine church".

Any church that is busy building and maintaining without going out for mission work may not be called a genuine church. Mind you "A genuine church always looks for a genuine pastor". No wonder many churches are busy looking for pastors of their type. Once you discovered that a pastor is not a genuine pastor, his members may be likewise or he may influence his member to be like him. That's why you wonder why some of the big churches lack focus in ministry, rather they always think on how to change their church paints, how to expand their church (even if the church can accommodates all the members), how to purchase their evangelical bus (even though the bus is not used for evangelism), how to fence their church and many more. One hardly you hear those churches thinking about evangelism or bringing evangelism or mission as their first agenda. Rob Frost further said "a church which has lost it's missionary vision is not an authentic New Testament church".

Evangelism is the church core task and the local church is the most appropriate place through which it should be done. Sadly, churches have lost their vision for this work and don't commit any resources to do it. In the same way, the local church does many things, but it's essential activity should be to leading, teaching, and nurturing people to Christ; all its other activities should always be secondary. Many churches don't seem to operate in this way.

There are many duties or church responsibilities that can be useful.

1. The church must be incarnational: Some Christians commutes several kilometers to church and attend worship; after service, they go back home again. Unfortunately these Christians become Sunday Christians. They don't relate with their neighbours to have a mid-week prayers; church with such commuters like these will not do the evangelism work effectively. If a church is to be effective in evangelism work, it must relate to the community in which it is set, and its congregation must constantly be building networks of relationship, service and witnessing within their locality.

    The first step is to encourage people to belong by

accepting them into your community and inviting them to journey with you. As they become part of us, they learn what Christian believe and how the behave as God's children. As they see the difference the Christian faith is making in their lives, they can decide to share their believe with others or not.

2. The church must be culturally relevant: Christians need to learn the language of those who cannot understand your right terminology. Often you are answering questions people are not asking and speaking big grammars that are beyond their understanding in a way that put them off. Many churches are so middle class in their language, dressing, culture and thinking, they are unapproachable to those from working class and backgrounds.

Those waiting to engage in church based evangelism should understand their target audience and know how to communicate in the way they will hear and understand. Most churches or pastors are careless about the language used in the church; that is why many churches have lost their church members to fraud pastors who are stealing members from other churches in order to enrich themselves. These fraud pastors or churches are careless about their member's spiritual standard; all they say is "thus says the Lord" while the Lord has said nothing, and it shall be well with you. It's important for the church to make a survey of the language that should be used in the church. If the church discover that there are some group of people who cannot understand their worship while the service is going on, the church should look for interpreter. And where there is no interpreter, then the church should consider opening a small church and ask someone who is spirit-fill and can speak their language very well to lead them.

I was a member of a Hausa speaking church where the church was having over 400 members men and women children exclusive. There were three categories of members in that church; some heard and spoke Hausa language, others had interest in starting an English speaking church while others don't hear or speak Hausa except English. The youth of that church required an English speaking church but the pastor was very selfish and greedy; thinking that he may lost some members to English speaking church without knowing that the church is for God; and that the primary task of the church is to reach the un-reached. The pastor rejected the youths idea because he did not know how to speak good English, for that, some members left the church to other churches while some the fell in the hands of fraud churches who are only after members money not their spiritual lives. Cultural relevant evangelism should not be over emphasized. If the church is offering form of worship that are too cerebral and text based, the message won't get through. The church life and outreach must be seemed to work and to be directly relevant to people's lives.

3.   The Church must reach the un-reach: many churches who think they are doing evangelism are just talking to themselves. "it takes great commitment and determination for a church to reach the un-reach". Evangelism to people who have never heard Christ message should be the highest priority for every church. Jesus commanded: Therefore, go and make disciples of all the nations, ... (Matthew 28:19-20) NLT.

Jesus' great commission is a task that every church must embark on, the church has forsaken her primary task and embark on physical and worldly project which have no regard on the side of our Lord and Saviour Jesus Christ. The church should know that making disciple of the un-reach people should be the first of all they have in mind; any church that is unable to win at least ten to fifteen unbelievers in a year is a deadly church. The church should every year set a budget or goal, of number of areas and people they will lead to Christ. One is always angry hearing a pastors saying that they have embarked on 15, 20, or 100 million building project; and all their offerings goes to this project. This reminds me when I was a student in one of the Nigerian Baptist Convention reputable Theological Institutions (Baptist Pastor School Jos, now Baptist College of Theology Jos). I went to one church seeking for financial assistance at Kaduna, it was unfortunate for me after I had introduced myself to the church pastor and explained to him the purpose of my coming. The church pastor said to me: "come, you see this building only at the foundation level, we had spend more than 5million naira"; because of that the church cannot help you but we will give N2000 to transport yourself back to Jos. This pastor did not even consider that I am under training and after studies I am going to the field "the work is plenty but the workers are few". He did not know that they had neglected or missed their vision as a church of mission and embarking on building mansion.

The church should know that they have a task that is beyond cathedral building, it is beyond making the best church on earth; but what the church should ask the question: "ARE WE BEST IN WINING SOULS AND PLANTING CHURCHES?" If not then, the church is a disgrace to Jesus and at a matter of urgency the church should seek the face of God and also go back to her primary assignment.

4. The church must preach the sound word: preaching is an act of wining combat. Unfortunately some churches become thieves and robbers stealing members of other churches instead of going to the world of darkness to win more souls for Christ. While in Jos, someone gave me a pamphlet and said: "Pastor, I am inviting you to our church service every Sunday 10:00am". When I came back sharing with other pastor who responded that "his wife ever visit a church and every Saturday that church pastor always invite her for Sunday service". Looking at these two experiences, you can see how foolish this person and the so-called pastor inviting another pastor and pastor's wife for every Sunday service in their church. Now, what did he want the pastor's wife to do? Did he want her to divorce her husband because of his church or want to cause crisis between them? That was why Paul said:

> People will be lovers of themselves, lovers of money, boastful, proud, abusive, disobedient to their parents, ungrateful, unholy, without love, unforgiving, slanderous, without self-control, brutal, not lovers of the good, treacherous, rash, conceited, lovers of pleasure rather than lovers of God- having a form of godliness but denying its power. Have nothing to do with them. They are the kind who worm their way into homes and gain

control over weak-willed women, who are loaded down with sins and are swayed by all kinds of evil desires, always learning but never able to acknowledge the truth. Just as Jannes and Jambres opposed Moses, so also these men oppose the truth-men of depraved minds, who, as far as the faith is concerned, are rejected. (2 Tim 3:2-9) NIV.

Many pastors have deviated from the true word of God; they no longer preach sound doctrine of the word because they need more members. Talking to a church member about not coming to church with un-decent dressing, she responded that: "Pastor there are many churches in the town that don't care about dressing because they say God is after our heart not dressing". These churches are everywhere and their target is to defocus the attention of some Christians in other churches and pull them to their church. Remember that everybody will give account of his or her deeds to God, whether good or bad.

CONCLUSION

Evangelism must have great priority in the life of the church, because the Master commissioned the church to do so. But it must go beyond special annual meetings efforts by selected soul-winners, and invitations given at every service. It must begin with you, church wide appreciation of good news of the Gospel and real concern for those who have not received Christ. Personal outreach on year-round basis, especially through the Sunday school, will demonstrate real and effective evangelism. This book affirms these convictions proves their effectiveness, and plead others in Christ name to practices them. SHALLOM!!!

BIBLIOGRAPHY

Gaines, S. Dobbins, <u>The Good News to Change Lives.</u>
Broadman Press

Holy Bible, <u>New International Version, Encyclopedia Edition</u>:
The Bible Society in Australia, Bill Noller International
Publishing Australia, 2007.
Holy Bible, New Living Translation

Holy Bible, Revised Standard Version

Judy, Pearsall and other, <u>Oxford Dictionary of English Second
Edition</u>: Sixth Edition, Oxford University Press, Great
Clarendon Street, Oxford Ox26DP, New York, 2010

Moyer, R. Lany. <u>How to Book on Personal Evangelism:</u> Krege
Publication, U.S.A 1998.

Nelson's Illustrated Bible Dictionary, Thomas Nelson
Publishers, Copyright (c) 1986

Rob Frost, <u>Sharing Jesus:</u> The Church most Urgent Task;
Scripture Union, 207-209 Qeensway, Bletchley, MK2
2EB, UK 2008.

Rob O'Callaghan, (former WMF staff member): What do we mean by 'Incarnational Methodology?' 6 May 2009.

Rogers, Glenn. <u>A basic Introduction to Missions and Missiology</u>: Mission and Ministry Resources Publication, 2003.

Wehmeier, Sally, <u>Oxford Advanced Leaner's Dictionary of Current English:</u> Sixth Edition, Oxford University Press, Great Clarendon Street, Oxford Ox2 6DP, New York, 2000

The New Unger's Bible Dictionary. Originally published by Moody Press of Chicago, Illinois. Copyright (c) 1988.

Nelson's Illustrated Bible Dictionary, Copyright (c) 1986, Thomas Nelson Publishers

Unknown Writer; <u>Types of Crisis That You Must Be Prepared For in Life</u>: http://www.magforliving.com/5-types-of-crisis-that-you-must-be-prepared-for-in-life/2/, 2013.

Chloe, Nicole Willson, Will, Flickety and 39 others, <u>How to Evangelize</u>: http://www.wikihow.com/Evangelize

❀

C. L. Kennedy, Ben Rubenstein, James Chang, Nicole
    Willson and 11 others: How to Be Generous:
    http://www.wikihow.com/Be-Generous

The New Unger's Bible Dictionary. Originally published by
    Moody Press of Chicago, Illinois. Copyright © 1988.

Your Dress Code: Clothing from an Islamic Perspective,
    http://newmuslimguide.com/en/your-dress-code/108